What a l

me

Monica Fearn

/ BookLeaf
Publishing

What a beautiful mess © 2023 Monica Fearn

All rights reserved.

Monica Fearn asserts the moral right to be
identified as the author of this work.

Presentation by *BookLeaf Publishing*

Web: www.bookleafpub.com

E-mail: info@bookleafpub.com

ISBN: 9789357744089

First edition 2023

I dedicate this book to me and to you

ACKNOWLEDGEMENT

How rare it is to fully acknowledge yourself in this world.

This book is for me, therefore I thank me.

PREFACE

Welcome to my jumbled, confusing, beautiful, haunted thoughts that have made me a poet.

I hope you enjoy

A simple breath

I take a deep breath in
And my body turns to stars.
Beaming in the twilight
A space so tranquil and vast.
As I float through the cosmos
The sun caresses me with its warmth.
I feel safe here
There's no sight of any storms.
I exhale out
And reality sets in.
Oh how I dream to be among the stars again.

Fight or flight

Shh. My beating heart
Rattling the cage, it's tearing apart.
Still. Breaths deafen my ears
In comes hope and out goes fears.
Stop. Mind's doing flips
Past to future it freely dips.
Silence. Focus on me
Loosening tension, set me free.

Deliciously human

Deep in my eyes
You'll find sweet candy skies.
Lollipops for raindrops
And dollymix galore.
Fluffy clouds made from marshmallow
Rainbow dust along the floor.
Flying saucers spinning frantically
Dropping sherbert all around.
Listen in carefully
How sweet is the sound.

Here Is good

How? Why?
When did I get this far?
A smooth U-turn back
A quick spin of the car.
Oh, you think it would be easy on this old dirt
track
No, the bumps will make you queasy
Are you sure to turn back?

There are three different paths to take my dear,
Backwards is familiar
But you'll never feel in gear..
Racing forwards is exciting
But the views will be unclear.
The last way that I'll propose
As for the other two you can dispose.
Why not step out of the car
Breathe in those scenic views
For each little step can be yours to choose.

Unlearning

This body that walks around,
Not me.
The voice that conducts a sound,
Not me.
A face that I paint and mask,
Not me.

Who am I
Where did I go
Was it all truth
Or was it all show
Can I ever be found
So deep in the ground

A whisper, it hits me
So powerful, so kind.
This is truth you have entered
For in this darkness you shall find
You cannot hide forever
Your truth will set you free.
I stop scrambling upwards
I accept and let it be.
The girl I know
She is inside.
She's scared, she's hurt

But uses love as her guide.
This girl I know
This is me
This quiet whisper will set me free.

Here right now, I can gladly say
This body that walks around
It's me.
The voice that conducts a sound
It's me.
This face whether painted or not
It's me.
Raw and real
I finally feel free.

Whole

I dream to be happy
No room for grief.
I strive for love
Hate dropped by my feet.
I wish to be confident
No shyness to be found.
Can I be all accepting
Through jealousy to the ground?

This person I want
This person is half.
The shadow will follow
Creating pain and mistrust.
Step into the dark
Invite it to your home.
For one to become whole
Light can't live alone.

Don't leave me

Slowly, I tremor
Depths I've never been before.
Helpless, mind racing
Feet jitter on the floor.
Am I invisible? Can they see me?
Not even left a clue.
Silent whispers, distant chatter
Confide in me too?
Are they okay?
I'm begging
That's all I need to know.
Are they lonely? Scared?
Times moving so slow.
Nothing matters anymore
Nothing matters at all.
As long as you are safe,
Everything else can fall.

Contortionist

She tried so hard to fit in
Squeezing into 'normality'.
Ending up completely exhausted
Feeling nothing, but a waste of space.
Until one day she realised
She was powerful and lovable just by being
herself.

Hare and the tortoise

Can slow and unsteady win the race too?

Grey

I want to be far away from here
I want to disappear.
Leave behind my friends and family,
So no one has to take care of me.
Let me hear the angels sing,
In the afterlife - my time will begin.

But is it really all or nothing
Is it really black or white?
Maybe I could spread my wings and put up a
little fight.
I don't have to please the world
I don't have to stand on my own two feet.
I just have to be here, right now. All I have to do
is be me.

It's going to be hard
To be sitting in this in-between.
Not black, not white, but grey
A place I have never been.

I am

I am loving, but am sometimes hateful.
I am excitable, but also fearful.
I am loyal, but can be flakey.
I am happy, but often sad.
I am forgiving, but sometimes it's hard for me.
I am fun, but also incredibly boring.
I am me.
I am whole.
I am wonderful.

Trigger

Sinking, drowning
I'm gasping for air.
Clenching, in pain
Can't remember my name.
Will I stay, will I fight
Or will I take flight.
Time watching, tick-tock
Get me out of this shock.

Perfection

She tried, yes she tried
Big leaps at a time.
Everyone applauded,
Yet she didn't feel rewarded.
The demons they crippled her,
All alone at night.
No one to help her distinguish the fight.
Never proud, never free
It felt impossible to just be.

One day she stopped fighting
The battle was lost.

But you'd never guess what happened
On that very same day.
All those fears and those worries
They vanished away.
She accepted her demons
Shook each of their hands.
Fighting is not the answer,
They aren't dragging you down.
They are giving you the chance
A choice for your life.
What's most important
And what causes you strife.

That same girl is now proud; and has never felt
more free,
She doesn't need applause
To be filled with glee.
That girl that I'm talking about,
That girl is me.

Walls

Years and years
I've spent building walls
Towering so high around me.
A place to keep me safe from hurt
So no-one could ever scar me.

Little did I know
This place I built, was the most toxic place of all
Worse than prison
It's hell on earth
With no-one that I can call.
No sentence is guaranteed
I might never see the light
No windows
No doors, to help me flee
I built this space too tight.

All I can do is scream and shout
My spark is slowly burning out.

No more to do but surrender
Time to wave the white flag
Peace.
Quiet.

At last.

My lungs bloom with air
Finally finding space to breathe.
My eyes start to flood with tears,
Allowing myself to grieve.

I won't be okay today,
Or tomorrow, or the next.
But I'll slowly chip away these walls
And I'll be alright in the end.

"Not bad"

Today I feel wild
Soaring high above.
Playful like a child
Heart flooding with love

Flow

Today I am high and bright.
A crest of a wave
Bathing in sunlight.
Tomorrow will I still be surfing?
Or tumbling, crashing
The dark seas, they're haunting.
Whichever, whatever
I'm still okay.
This journey is mine
So I'll take my sweet time.

Who am I?

When I lay down the chatter
Feeling my way into an answer
I realise
I am merely nothing.

Nothing that is aware of everything.

The Wrong Therapist

Hello, he speaks in a strange-sounding voice,
Oh God, why me, this wasn't my choice.
Insides so numb,
Feel brittle as a crumb.
I'm sad,
Yes I'm mad.
But wouldn't you be too?
Is it me, only me
Or is it sometimes you?
Do I trust you with my secrets?
A stranger I've just met.
Do I open up my wounds?
Though I feel this is a threat
It's the only way to heal you say,
Dig deeper inside.
How can this be possible?
When my blood's already dried.

A quote I like

The only way to learn is to live
-     Matt Haig

Milton Keynes UK
Ingram Content Group UK Ltd.
UKHW020655200923
429044UK00015B/456

9 789357 744089